VITAL TO EARTH!
Keystone Species Explained

T0011188

PRAIRIE DOGS
IN THEIR ECOSYSTEMS

by Sophie Christopher

BEARPORT
PUBLISHING

Minneapolis, Minnesota

Credits
Cover and title page, © HenkBentlage/iStock; 4–5, © Cavan/Adobe Stock; 7, © David Butler/iStock;
9, © Dorling Kindersley/Getty; 10, © Wirestock/iStock; 10–11, © Dorling Kindersley ltd/Alamy; 12–13,
© robertharding/Alamy; 14–15, © Don Johnston_MA/Alamy; 17, © Семен Саливанчук/Adobe
Stock; 18–19, © Aynia Brennan/Shutterstock; 20–21, © USGS/Alamy; 22–23, © FotoLesnik/iStock; 23, ©
Sergey-AND-Marina/iStock; 24–25, © sekernas/iStock; 26–27, © Ivan Kuzmin/Alamy; 28, © Petr Bonek/
Shutterstock; 29T, © Dusan Stankovic/iStock; 29TM, © shironosov/iStock; 29M, © Jbryson/iStock; 29BM,
© Mongkolchon Akesin/iStock; 29B, © Ababsolutum/iStock.

Bearport Publishing Company Product Development Team
President: Jen Jenson; Director of Product Development: Spencer Brinker; Managing Editor: Allison Juda;
Associate Editor: Naomi Reich; Associate Editor: Tiana Tran; Art Director: Colin O'Dea; Designer: Elena
Klinkner; Designer: Kayla Eggert; Product Development Assistant: Owen Hamlin

STATEMENT ON USAGE OF GENERATIVE ARTIFICIAL INTELLIGENCE
Bearport Publishing remains committed to publishing high-quality nonfiction books. Therefore, we
restrict the use of generative AI to ensure accuracy of all text and visual components pertaining to a
book's subject. See BearportPublishing.com for details.

Library of Congress Cataloging-in-Publication Data

Names: Christopher, Sophie, author.
Title: Prairie dogs in their ecosystems / by Sophie Christopher.
Description: Minneapolis, Minnesota : Bearport Publishing Company, [2024] |
   Series: Vital to Earth! Keystone species explained | Includes
   bibliographical references and index.
Identifiers: LCCN 2023040969 (print) | LCCN 2023040970 (ebook) | ISBN
   9798889166313 (library binding) | ISBN 9798889166382 (paperback) | ISBN
   9798889166443 (ebook)
Subjects: LCSH: Prairie dogs--Juvenile literature.
Classification: LCC QL737.R68 C4965 2024 (print) | LCC QL737.R68 (ebook)
   | DDC 599.36/7--dc23/eng/20230908
LC record available at https://lccn.loc.gov/2023040969
LC ebook record available at https://lccn.loc.gov/2023040970

For more information, write to Bearport Publishing, 5357 Penn Avenue South, Minneapolis, MN 55419.

Contents

Prairie Dogs at Work

It's a quiet day in a grassy field. A hawk soars above, scanning the area for something to eat. Down below, a snake slithers into a burrow made by another, and a bison scares off a hungry coyote.

Suddenly, a furry little critter stands up and lets out a high-pitched call. Hundreds of prairie dogs pop up from holes and start digging and eating. The work these animals do shapes **grasslands** from the ground up. Prairie dogs are vital to their **ecosystems**.

There are five **species** of prairie dogs. They live throughout the grasslands of North America, from Canada to northern Mexico. Despite their name, these animals are actually ground squirrels, not dogs.

A Key Animal

Prairie dogs are a keystone species—a kind of plant or animal that is crucial to supporting an entire community of life within an area. A keystone species shapes the land or helps balance the populations of plants and animals in a way that benefits everything in the environment.

The ways prairie dogs eat, dig, and communicate with one another all work to help the rest of life in the grassland. Without them, the soil might break down, grasses could fail, and both predators and prey across the habitat would suffer.

Grasslands are areas where grasses are the most common type of plant life. Grasslands do not get a lot of rain, but they get more rain than deserts.

Most grasslands
are relatively flat.

Who Let the Dogs Out?

Using their sharp claws, prairie dogs dig burrows across grasslands. These sheltered homes protect them from bad weather and predators. Each burrow is made up of a maze of tunnels and rooms that typically house an adult male, three or four adult females, and several prairie dog pups.

The prairie dogs dig tunnels to join a huge network of burrows. As individual families connect their homes, they become part of a prairie dog town. Sometimes these **colonies** are massive. The largest known prairie dog town was bigger than the state of West Virginia!

Many animals that cannot dig their own holes make their homes in active or **abandoned** prairie dog burrows. Jackrabbits, snakes, salamanders, bugs, and even burrowing owls hunker down in prairie dog burrows.

Toil for the Soil

All of the prairie dogs' digging helps the grassland soil. The constant burrowing loosens and mixes the upper layer of earth. This lets in the water, air, and **nutrients** that prairie plants need to grow. The roots of the plants then hold the soil in place, so it does not blow away in the wind or wash away in flooding rains. Healthy growth also helps keep the **grazers** of the ecosystem healthy.

Good grassland soil produces plants that keep populations of bison and elk healthy. Then, they can more easily give birth to and raise healthy babies.

How Low Can It Grow?

The grasses that prairie dog burrowing helps grow are also their source of food. The animals munch away, keeping the grasses around their burrows short. This allows prairie dogs to spot predators more easily. It also makes eating easier for other grassland creatures. Low grasses let birds of prey more easily spot small animals as they fly above. Down below, smaller birds build nests and feed on the bugs that live in the rich soil uncovered by thin grasses. Keeping grasses low also gives more room for small shrubs and flowering plants to grow, offering grazers a wider range of healthy dining options.

Prairie dogs do a lot of eating. They also do a lot of pooping. But this waste does not go to waste! It's good for grassland soil.

Prairie dogs eat mostly grasses. Ocassionaly, they also snack on bugs.

Prairie Dog Dinners

Sometimes, prairie dogs become the prey they have made more visible.

Coyotes, bobcats, hawks, and badgers all eat prairie dogs.

A wide variety of animals hunt prairie dogs. So many predators chow down on these small animals that they are sometimes called the chicken nuggets of the prairie! Prairie dogs are one of the only sources of food for the black-footed ferret, an **endangered** grassland species. Without the prairie dog, the ferret would die off, and many other grassland creatures would go hungry.

Prairie dogs have developed calls that warn their colony members—and other grassland neighbors—of nearby predators. Their barks and yelps can describe a predator's size, color, shape, and speed!

Beating the Heat

By taking care of their ecosystems, prairie dogs are actually helping to cool down our warming planet. We burn **fossil fuels** to power our cars, homes, and businesses. Every time we do, we release a gas called **carbon dioxide** that traps heat around Earth and causes temperatures to rise. This extra warmth is changing our **climate** and causing unusual weather, monster storms, and severe droughts. But healthy grasslands keep our planet cool! Their soil and plants store a third of the world's heat-trapping carbon.

The changing climate is impacting the grasslands where prairie dogs live. Grassland habitats are getting hotter and drier. This makes it harder for some plants to grow.

Transportation is the leading source of carbon dioxide emissions in the United States.

Prairie Pests?

Even though prairie dogs are key to their ecosystems, they have long been under attack from humans. In the 1800s, European farmers and ranchers moved to the North American grasslands. The healthy soil the prairie dogs created was great for farming. But farmers were afraid the animals would feed on their crops and the grasses they needed for **livestock**. They also worried that their cattle, sheep, and horses would step in burrow holes and break their legs. Settlers started shooting and poisoning prairie dogs. The little creatures began disappearing from the grasslands.

It is estimated that before 1800, there were more than five billion prairie dogs across the grasslands of North America.

Prairie Dog Disease

As if being hunted and poisoned weren't bad enough, prairie dogs are also threatened by a deadly disease. Sylvatic **plague** was first brought to North America about 100 years ago by flea-bitten rats carried from Asia on trading ships.

The disease spreads quickly among **rodents**, including prairie dogs. If a single prairie dog gets sick, the disease can spread and wipe out the whole colony within two weeks. Between poisonings, shootings, and diseases, the prairie dog population has dropped by about 98 percent over the last 200 years.

Infected prairie dogs can spread sylvatic plague to other grassland animals, too. Badgers, weasels, ferrets, bobcats, and coyotes can also get very sick from this disease.

Scientists are trying
to save prairie dogs
from the plague.
They leave out pieces
of food covered in a
vaccine.

When Colonies Collapse

When prairie dogs are no longer a part of their prairie, the ecosystem collapses. Without the digging prairie dogs, the soil becomes hard and dry. It can no longer hold as much water. This makes it difficult for new plants to grow, damaging the ecosystem's most important source of food and shelter.

Grazers strip the area of the plants that remain. Then, without the roots of plants to hold it in place, soil can easily be swept away by wind or water.

Taller woody shrubs and trees move in to areas stripped of grasses. Birds that build nests and feed in short grasses must leave. Birds of prey struggle to spot food on the ground through the taller plants.

Other Animals Suffer

Plant and animal species in a grassland suffer without prairie dogs. The creatures that used prairie dog burrows for their homes are left without shelter if the rodents leave.

The black-footed ferret nearly went **extinct** when prairie dog populations shrank. It is still one of the most endangered mammals in North America. The swift fox, which also eats prairie dogs, is in trouble without this important food source.

With prairie dog numbers dropping, the short grass in the ecosystem is disappearing. As a result, grassland bird populations are declining faster than any other birds in North America.

There are only a few hundred black-footed ferrets left in the wild.

Learning to Live Together

After seeing what has happened to grasslands without their keystone species, some people have decided to take action.

Conservationists are working to change negative views of prairie dogs. They teach people how important prairie dogs are and how humans can live together with the animals. Instead of killing them, more farmers and ranchers have been trapping and **relocating** prairie dogs, keeping whole families together. After all, life on the grasslands depends on these little critters.

Some prairie dog species are considered threatened or endangered. This gives them some legal protections. Still, many local governments support killing prairie dogs if they interfere with farming.

Save the Prairie Dogs

Plants and animals across the grasslands depend on prairie dogs. So when they are in danger, the whole ecosystem is threatened. Luckily, there are some things we can do to protect this keystone species and help it in its life-giving work.

Tell your friends, family, and classmates about how important prairie dogs are. Make posters, give out flyers, and write up information to share about these keystone species.

Write to local leaders to ask them to make it illegal to harm prairie dogs.

Support groups trying to keep grassland areas wild. The more land we take from prairie dogs, the harder it will be for them to survive.

When visiting grasslands or any natural areas, be sure to do your part to keep them healthy. Stay on the path and give any wildlife you see plenty of space.

Keep your pets away from wild animals. Cats and dogs can chase, attack, and even kill prairie dogs if they are allowed to get close to the wild animals.

Glossary

abandoned left empty or unused

carbon dioxide a greenhouse gas given off when fossil fuels are burned

climate the usual, expected weather in an area

colonies groups of animals that live together

conservationists people who take care of the natural world

ecosystems communities of animals and plants that depend on one another to live

endangered close to dying off completely

extinct a kind of plant or animal that has died out

fossil fuels energy sources, such as coal, oil, and gas, that are made from the remains of plants and animals that died millions of years ago

grasslands biomes marked by wide, open areas of land with low-growing grasses and plants

grazers animals that eat plants from the ground

infected filled with harmful germs

livestock animals, such as horses, sheep, and cows, raised on farms or ranches

nutrients vitamins, minerals, and other substances needed by living things for health and growth

plague a disease that causes death and spreads quickly

relocating moving to another area

rodents small mammals that have long front teeth

species groups that plants and animals are divided into, according to similar characteristics

Read More

Bell, Samantha. *Park Life from Dinosaur to Prairie Dogs (National Park Adventures).* Ann Arbor, MI: Cherry Lake Publishing, 2024.

Bergin, Raymond. *Grassland Life Connections (Life on Earth! Biodiversity Explained).* Minneapolis: Bearport Publishing, 2023.

Bodden, Valerie. *Prairie Dogs (Amazing Animals).* Mankato, MN: Creative Education, 2023.

Learn More Online

1. Go to **www.factsurfer.com** or scan the QR code below.

2. Enter "**Keystone Prairie Dogs**" into the search box.

3. Click on the cover of this book to see a list of websites.

Index

About the Author

Sophie Christopher lives in Brooklyn, New York, where she writes and goes to the local park every day it's warm out. Although she's very familiar with squirrels, she's never met a prairie dog. But she'd really like to one day.